Visions of Golf

Visions of Golf

A CELEBRATION OF THE WORK OF

THE ALLSPORT PHOTOGRAPHIC AGENCY.

THE WORLD'S FINEST

GOLF PHOTOGRAPHY.

KENSINGTON WEST
PRODUCTIONS

First published in 1994 by
Kensington West Productions Ltd
5 Cattle Market, Hexham
Northumberland NE46 1NJ

A CIP catalogue record for this book is available from the British Library

ISBN 1 871349 37 0

Editors: David Cannon and Nick Edmund

Editorial Contributors: Peter Dobereiner, Robert Green, John Hopkins, Mitchell Platts, Rick Reilly, Spencer Robinson

Picture Research: Andrew Redington
Picture Research (Asia): Prism

Designed by Rob Kelland at Allsport

Origination by Colour Systems, London
Printed in Italy by Rotolito Lombarda S.p.A.

Ernie Els silhouette (half-title page)
PHOTOGRAPH BY MICHAEL COOPER

Robert Karlsson (frontispiece)
PHOTOGRAPH BY STEPHEN MUNDAY

Nick Faldo (title page)
PHOTOGRAPH BY DAVID CANNON

Greg Norman (left)
PHOTOGRAPH BY DAVID CANNON

FOREWORD

by Gene Sarazen

VISIONS OF GOLF... if only there had been an Allsport photographer standing behind the 15th green at Augusta in 1935! Was it really 60 years ago? The double-eagle: somebody called it, 'the shot heard around the world'. It was an exciting moment, all right, and I was able to see it all happen before my eyes, but as my ball disappeared into the hole for a two I was still not sure that I would win the Masters – one mistake over the last three holes and it would have been a double eagle without any feathers!

As a boy I used to caddie at the Apawamis Country Club in Rye, New York. I started playing golf when I was about nine years old and now I have a lifetime of memories. Both golfers and photographers are fortunate in that they get to travel the world. I really enjoyed playing in Australia, Japan and Europe. Not many people are aware of this but whenever I played in tournaments or matches overseas I used to write to Bobby Jones. I would tell him about everything I saw; I believe I wrote him 35 letters in all.

It is a pity Jones couldn't have been at Troon in 1973 when I holed-in-one at the Postage Stamp. That is another great memory. I was in a three ball with Fred Daly and Max Faulkner – the fellow who always played in knickers. The hole-in-one came in the first round and hardly anybody was watching. On the second day there were thousands of people crowded on the dunes surrounding the green. I hit my tee shot into the bunker and from there I could just see the top of the flag – but the ball jumped in for a two! My putter was never used on that hole.

You have a picture of me playing from a bunker and I guess that's appropriate as I am credited with inventing the sand iron. The pros these days seem happier playing out of traps than from rough. I believe that if you took the sand iron out of their bag scores would be at least five strokes higher over 72 holes.

I have watched all the great players over the years and seen many of the great tournaments. It has always been my dream to bring champions from all over the world together and in November 1994 I am honoured to be hosting the first Gene Sarazen World Open Championship at The Legends at Chateau Elan Golf Club in Atlanta, Georgia. There will be a truly international field and I regard it as my contribution to the legacy of golf. I hope it enriches the sport: it is a beautiful and magical game and the pictures in this book capture much of the beauty and much of the magic.

GENE SARAZEN

MARCO ISLAND, FLORIDA

Gene Sarazen at The Masters

PHOTOGRAPH BY DAVID CANNON

Severiano Ballesteros in full flight during the 1988 Open Championship

PHOTOGRAPH BY DAVID CANNON

INTRODUCTION

by David Cannon

ALLSPORT'S BEGINNINGS can be traced to a single photograph taken in 1968. In his foreword to this book Gene Sarazen reflects, 'If only there had been an Allsport photographer standing behind the 15th green at Augusta in 1935!' An impossibility, sadly, but a further 33 years into the century Tony Duffy, the founder of Allsport, was poised adjacent to the Long Jump pit at the 1968 Mexico Olympics. Duffy captured a magnificent picture of Bob Beamon's famous leap. The rest, as they say, is history. With due deference to Sarazen's 'shot heard around the world', this was the shot seen around the world.

Duffy's photograph – not to mention his initiative – set a standard of excellence which to this day every Allsport photographer seeks to aspire. In celebration of the company's 25th anniversary Visions of Sport was published; now Visions of Golf follows to celebrate Allsport's long association with the world of golf.

It is said that some photographers are born with a camera in their hand but for me it was a set of golf clubs. At the age of two I was despatching a dozen of my father's unwrapped Dunlop 65s into the dense rhododendron bushes at the back of our Ascot home. This love for golf has never diminished.

I played the British amateur circuit in the early 1970s and although I enjoyed limited success I have always placated myself with the thought that I was never likely to succeed against such contemporaries as Nick Faldo,

Mark James and Sandy Lyle! In May 1976 I entered a pro-am at my home club, The Leicestershire and had the amazing fortune to be drawn with an unknown Spaniard called Severiano Ballesteros. Again, the rest, as they say, is history!

That memory of seeing the youthful Seve in full flight has never left me and since becoming a golf photographer (I picked up my first SLR camera in 1978 and joined Allsport in 1983) I have been lucky to capture many images of this majestic player, some of which still send chills down my spine when I recall the excitement surrounding these moments.

In any one calendar year Allsport's London and Los Angeles offices will cover nearly 100 golf tournaments from all over the world. Recently we obtained unique access to the sports library of the Hulton Deutsch Collection, introducing us to a marvellous variety of black and white photographs of the early legends of golf, including Bobby Jones and Gene Sarazen. The addition of this historical collection to the finest contemporary library has, I believe, given Allsport the most comprehensive golf library in the world.

Visions of Golf would not have been possible without the support of United Distillers Asia. Together with United Distillers in London, they are perhaps the greatest supporters of international golf. I thank them sincerely on behalf of everyone at Allsport.

DAVID CANNON

LEGENDS

Arnold Palmer plays from the Church Pews bunker during his final US Open at Oakmont in 1994

PHOTOGRAPH BY GARY NEWKIRK

LEGENDS

by Peter Dobereiner

WILLIAM ST CLAIR of Roslin may have been a legendary figure in his day. He is the chap with the big nose, red coat and absurdly closed stance whose portrait by Sir George Chalmers adorns 99.7% of golf clubs in print form. He was captain of the Honourable Company of Edinburgh Golfers back in the 18th century and he was possessed of such uncanny skill as to give rise to the superstition that he had done a deal with a witch. In return for helping her to get into parliament she transmogrified herself into his golf ball. When struck from the teeing ground she flew like the breeze straight and far down the fairway and he had only to give her a tap with his putter and she rolled obediently into the hole. The stuff of legends, indeed.

But the game was not widely documented, nor widely played, for another hundred years and the start of the Open Championship in 1860 is perhaps a suitable point for identifying the legendary figures of golf. Such a process must perforce be subjective and arbitrary and it would be a dull old world indeed if your list of legends coincided with mine, particularly as I propose to limit my selection to a very narrow definition. Ever since 1860 the golfing public has operated a mysterious process of consensus, like the way a flock of birds changes direction with each individual turning simultaneously without any apparent signal, to select one man as the role model for what a golfer should be, in his play, in his deportment and in his dress.

Old Tom Morris was the first candidate and the only thing about him that the golfing community did not take as an example to be followed was his legendary beard. Then Harry Vardon was appointed by oxymoronic silent acclamation, in the United States as well as at home. The international nature of the game's legend-in-residence was reinforced when the American amateur, Bobby Jones, was appointed as the ne plus ultra of golf.

The succession then passed to the present incumbent, a person who has been voted the athlete of the century and the best known, and best loved, man in the world: Arnold Palmer. Since he is the best known man in the world I will not waste your time and mine by telling you about his fabulous career, some 90-odd victories around the world and counting. But it might be of some small interest to reflect on the qualities and circumstances which made him our unanimous choice.

Palmer's main and most impressive trick is to create the illusion that he is one of us, just a regular guy who likes to sit around the locker room chewing the fat with the boys and drinking beer straight from the can. He even manages to carry that impression out onto the golf course. Stand close to Greg Norman when

Gene Sarazen congratulates Greg Norman on his 1993 Open Championship triumph at Royal St George's ("Legends", pages 10-11)

PHOTOGRAPH BY DAVID CANNON

he lets rip with the driver and you are left in no doubt that you are in the presence of Superman. The way you hit the ball bears no resemblance whatever to the way he hits the ball. With Arnie the experience is not all that alien. His swing is not a thing of classic beauty so you've got something in common with him straight off. His shot follows your usual line, further maybe but still into the woods. Now, again like you, he takes a dirty great hack at the ball. For some reason your ball always hits a tree and rebounds deeper into the woods but Palmer gets lucky, finds a gap and lands on the green. So what is the difference between your customary double-bogey and his normal birdie? A bit of luck; that's all.

The distinction that separates Palmer from the rest of us can be calculated rather more scientifically by the use of advanced mathematics. From observation we know that out of every thousand people who take up golf only one becomes proficient enough to turn pro. It is a matter of statistical record that only one in a hundred professionals becomes good enough to make a living on the Tour. Furthermore, of those successful touring pros fewer than one in a hundred goes on to become a multiple winner of the major championships. That makes Palmer a man in ten million, not exactly a run of the mill, ordinary bloke like the rest of us.

Mind you, that is how he started. His father got a job with the construction crew which built the 9-hole Latrobe Country Club in Pennsylvania. Deacon Palmer stayed on as greenkeeper and club professional. In due course Arnold became an assistant professional. These days he reflects that his father was unduly hard on him. As to that, who are we to judge? By his own admission Arnold was for ever locking up the shop and nipping out to hit balls. Most likely he had a few clips around the ear coming to him. What is certain is that by the time Arnold flew the nest he had a good grip, a thorough knowledge of the rules along with an unswerving devotion to their observance in both the letter and the spirit, and the zeal of a missionary in upholding the sporting heritage of the game, all these being the gifts of his father.

His timing was good in that he happened along just when television was becoming a household necessity. He had the build of a middleweight boxer, with broad shoulders tapering down to hips so narrow that his pants would not stay up, constantly requiring him to give them a hitch. He was personable, affable and colourful and those qualities, combined with his devastating good looks and buccaneering style of play, made him an instant television star as well as a sporting hero. He was the son every father wished he'd had; and the boyfriend every mother wished for her daughter. Some of the mothers had other wishes for him, as also did many of their daughters. I could never understand what the women saw in him but I would have killed for a crate of the stuff. Single-handedly he turned professional golf into a major spectator sport. Mind you, it did not hurt that his close friend, President Dwight D Eisenhower, was a golf nut.

When the passing years eventually undermined his putting stroke and took him out of contention he was still top of every popularity poll and too hot a property for the game to lose. So they invented the Senior Tour for him. Thanks to Arnold Palmer his

contemporaries suddenly found that the grass was even greener over the crest of that dreaded hill. They had a new lease of competitive life and what amounted to a munificent pension scheme. And when successive annual drafts of 50-year-old rookies pushed Palmer aside they invented the Super Senior Tour in order to retain the exceptional power of his magnetic personality to pull in the fans and the sponsors.

For five decades golfers all over the world have strived to live up to the example of Arnold Palmer. Because of that example golf has remained clean and honest, a vital consideration for the health of a game which depends on morality and sportsmanship for its very existence. There is a school of thought which argues that in return for the entertainment which Palmer has provided golf has made him rich and famous. Therefore Palmer and golf are all square. I disagree. Knowing something of the contributions he has made in time and effort in trying to uphold the game's traditional standards, mostly behind the scenes, in addition to the example he has set in public, I believe that golf is and will always remain deeply in his debt.

Arnold Palmer, portrait of a legend

PHOTOGRAPH BY GARY NEWKIRK

Gene Sarazen was the first golfer to win all four of golf's modern grandslam events: The Masters, the US Open, the Open Championship and the USPGA. This photograph (right) was taken at his home on Marco Island, Florida in 1994.

PHOTOGRAPH BY DAVID CANNON

Ben Hogan and Sam Snead dominated golf in the 1940s and 1950s; their rivalry was intense but when they joined forces to represent their country, as in the 1956 Canada Cup at Wentworth (above left) they were almost invincible.

'Who's going to finish second, fellas?' was one of Walter Hagen's favourite quips. When it came to head to head competition the answer was invariably his opponent. Hagen, pictured (below left) was the supreme matchplay golfer, winning the USPGA Championship (in the years before it became a strokeplay event) four times in succession.

In 1930, aged just 28, Bobby Jones (right) retired from competitive golf after capturing golf's original grandslam of the US Open, US Amateur, Open Championship and British Amateur all in the same year. Of the 31 Major championships he entered, he won 13 and was placed first or second 19 times. Adored in Great Britain almost as much as he was worshipped in America, Jones won the last three Open Championships he played in, including, the 1927 championship at his beloved St Andrews.

PHOTOGRAPHS BY ALLSPORT/HULTON DEUTSCH

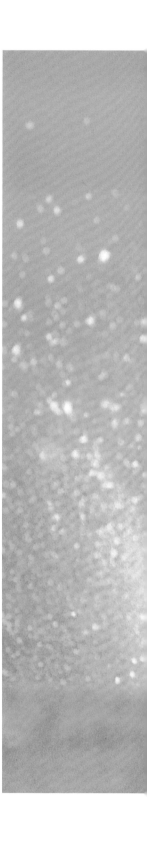

*A*rnold Palmer, Gary Player and Jack Nicklaus: they were known as the 'Big Three' in the 1960s, although Nicklaus was still winning Major championships in the 1980s. All three are pictured at Augusta and it was at The Masters that they gained many of their greatest triumphs. Player, the first overseas winner of the famous Green Jacket won three times, Palmer won four times and Nicklaus has achieved a record six Masters victories.

Arnold Palmer (above)
Photograph by David Cannon

Gary Player (left)
Photograph by David Cannon

Jack Nicklaus (right)
Photograph by David Cannon

*B*amboozled: a pensive Watson and a perplexed Trevino. Perhaps the caption should be,
  'Swap you one of my Masters victories for one of your PGA Championships?' Only Gene Sarazen,
  Ben Hogan, Gary Player and Jack Nicklaus have won all four of golf's grandslam events.
  They may have fourteen major titles between them, but five time Open champion Watson has never
  won the USPGA Championship and 'Super Mex' has never triumphed at Augusta.

Tom Watson at the 1992 Masters (above)

Lee Trevino at Shoal Creek in the 1984 USPGA Championship (right)

Photographs by David Cannon

*S*ome children build sand castles on the beach; others hit pebbles
across the sand with rusty 3-irons. Some children grow up
to be ordinary mortals, others grow to be legends.

Severiano Ballesteros at the 1987 Ryder Cup, Muirfield Village (left)
Severiano Ballesteros returns to the beach at Pedrena (above)

PHOTOGRAPHS BY DAVID CANNON

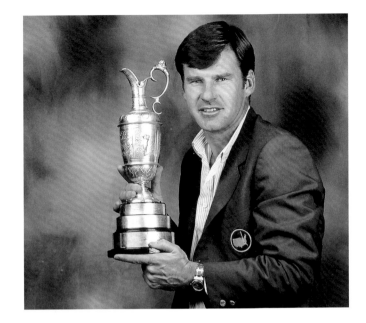

*T*he Faldo collection.

He is a perfectionist,
he is misunderstood and
he is the greatest British
golfer since Harry Vardon.
Nick Faldo is the only
player in history to have
won The Masters at
Augusta and the Open
Championship at St
Andrews in the same
calendar year.

Nick Faldo amidst the
pampas grass during a
Pringle shoot at Sun City
(above left)

Nick Faldo wins the 1992
Open Championship at
Muirfield (below left)

In 1990 Nick Faldo
conquered St Andrews
and Augusta (above right)

PHOTOGRAPHS BY DAVID CANNON

Nick Faldo and the pursuit
of excellence, testing his
overall body fitness at the
British Olympic Association
Medical Centre (right)

PHOTOGRAPH BY GARY M PRIOR

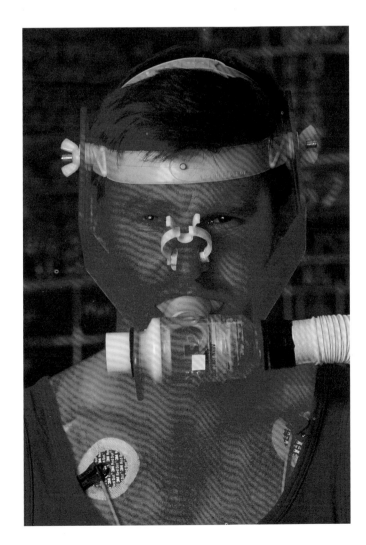

The only man who could have out-charged a charging Arnold Palmer:
Greg Norman, alias the Great White Shark. Although he has occasionally
flattered to deceive in Major championships – he is the only player to
have lost play-offs in all four grandslam events – nobody can bring
a golf course to its knees the way Norman can. He has scored 62s
at Glen Abbey and Doral's Blue Monster, 63s at St Andrews, Sawgrass,
Turnberry and Tryall and 64s at Augusta, Troon and Royal St George's.

Greg Norman blasts from the rough at Tryall in Jamaica
during the 1992 Johnnie Walker World Championship (left)
PHOTOGRAPH BY DAVID CANNON

Greg Norman portrait (above)
PHOTOGRAPH BY STEPHEN MUNDAY

*T*hey may not be perceived as legends in the West, but in Japan Masashi 'Jumbo' Ozaki, Isao Aoki and Ayako Okamoto are regarded as nothing less than golfing icons.

'Jumbo' Ozaki (right)
PHOTOGRAPH BY DAVID CANNON

Isao Aoki (above)
PHOTOGRAPH BY GARY NEWKIRK

Ayako Okamoto (far right)
PHOTOGRAPH BY GARY NEWKIRK

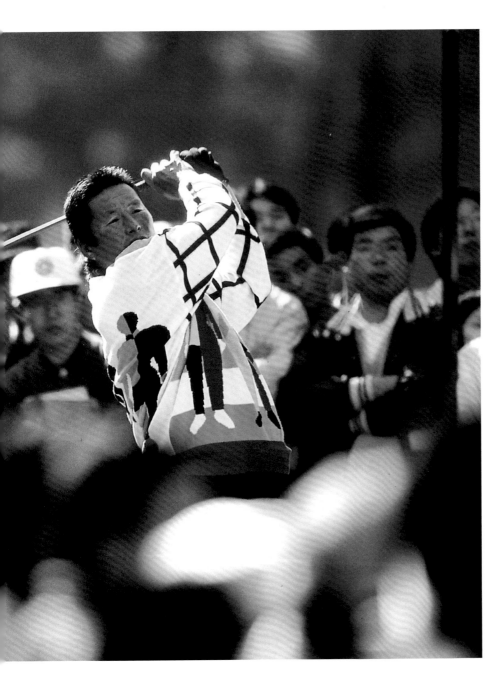

Just as there are golfing heroes, so there are golfing heroines. For Arnold Palmer read Nancy Lopez and for Severiano Ballesteros read Laura Davies. Between them, these four players revolutionised golf in America and Europe. Which two things do they have in common? Genius and charisma.

Nancy Lopez (above)

Laura Davies (right)

Photographs by David Cannon

THE MAJORS

Severiano Ballesteros birdies his final hole in the 1984 Open at St Andrews (above and overleaf)

Photographs by David Cannon

THE MAJORS

by Robert Green

THE FIRST MAJOR championship I attended in what we journalists like to call a working capacity was the 1976 Open at Royal Birkdale. That was the Open won, ultimately serenely, by Johnny Miller and lost, ever gloriously, by a 19 year-old Spaniard called Severiano Ballesteros.

It would be inaccurate to say that Seve – as he has become widely know in shorthand, as if, like Pele, he had no need for a second name – emerged from total obscurity during that flaming summer week in Southport, for he had topped the Continental Order of Merit the previous season, but until that championship began, few people had any appropriate conception of the formidable array of talents possessed by this prodigy.

In fact, Ballesteros lost that Open with his profligacy, and also his inexperience. Starting the final round two shots ahead of Miller, he soon proceeded to squander shots spectacularly and with alacrity, only to start picking them up with almost equal rapidity when his chance of victory had vanished but the possibility of being runner-up with Jack Nicklaus remained. The audaciously subtle chip-and-run shot to the last green, with which he secured his final birdie, has become the stuff of golfing legend.

Ballesteros has since won the Open three times – at Royal Lytham in 1979 and 1988

and, as pictured here, over the storied Old Course at St Andrews in 1984.

They say that every picture tells a story, and this one does with a vibrancy rarely matched in the comparatively undemonstrative sporting world of professional golf. It depicts Ballesteros the instant after his ball has toppled into the hole on the final green of the final round in that 1984 Open, its disappearance having been perpetrated by the deft execution of a right-to-left uphill breaking putt of some 12 feet.

In ordinary circumstances, an accomplished putter – and Ballesteros is manifestly one of the most accomplished in the history of golf – would fancy his chances of sinking such a putt on a fairly regular basis. But these were extraordinary circumstances.

With two holes of the championship to play, Ballesteros had been on 11 under par and tied for the lead with Tom Watson, the defending champion and his only rival for the accolade of then being the best golfer in the game. Ballesteros was paired with Bernhard Langer, Watson was with Ian Baker-Finch, the third-round leader, in the final match.

When Seve made his par four at the notoriously savage 17th, the 'Road Hole', the first time he had managed that much all week, the advantage almost perceptibly passed to him. Sure enough, Watson faltered, following a

Vast crowds gather around the 18th green of the Olympic Club, San Francisco during the 1987 US Open ("The Majors", pages 32-33)

PHOTOGRAPH BY DAVID CANNON

good drive with a misjudged second shot that finished on the eponymous road, perilously close to the wall. That was the predicament the great American faced as Ballesteros, after a solid drive and an excellent pitch, stood over that putt on the 18th green.

I explain all this in order to emphasise the prosaic truth that Ballesteros did not know that when his putt went in, he had won the Open. For all he knew, Watson might par the 17th and birdie the 18th, too.

Forget such niceties. Of course he knew he had won the Open. We all knew. There was no way fate would let it have been otherwise. Watson duly bogeyed the 17th and parred the 18th and that was officially that.

Ballesteros always refers to the putt as "the happiest moment in my golfing career". For those of us around the green that momentous Sunday who were only vicariously involved in its deliverance, it will forever remain one of the most memorable.

To win the Open over the Old Course at St Andrews, to beat his great adversary, Watson, and to do so with the singularly compelled elan that Ballesteros has brought to the game for nearly 20 years – that is why the moment captured in this picture sequence will enrich the annals of golfing lore into the next century and beyond.

Robert Green is the Editor of Golf World, UK

The bravest six foot putt that Ian Woosnam will ever hole. Welsh glory at Augusta as Woosnam follows Scotland's Sandy Lyle and England's Nick Faldo to secure Britain's fourth successive victory in The Masters.

Ian Woosnam wins the 1991 Masters

PHOTOGRAPH BY STEPHEN MUNDAY

"Winning the 1994 Masters meant that I had achieved one of the goals of my life, and this photograph is a beautiful memory of that moment"

JOSÉ-MARIA OLAZABAL

It was the year golf's Young Pretenders came of age. José-Maria Olazabal finally won his first Major title when he triumphed in the 1994 Masters at Augusta and South African Ernie Els won a three way play-off in the US Open at Oakmont to become the championship's youngest winner since 1976.

José-Maria Olazabal at The 1994 Masters (left)

Ernie Els raises the US Open trophy at Oakmont, 1994 (above)

PHOTOGRAPHS BY DAVID CANNON

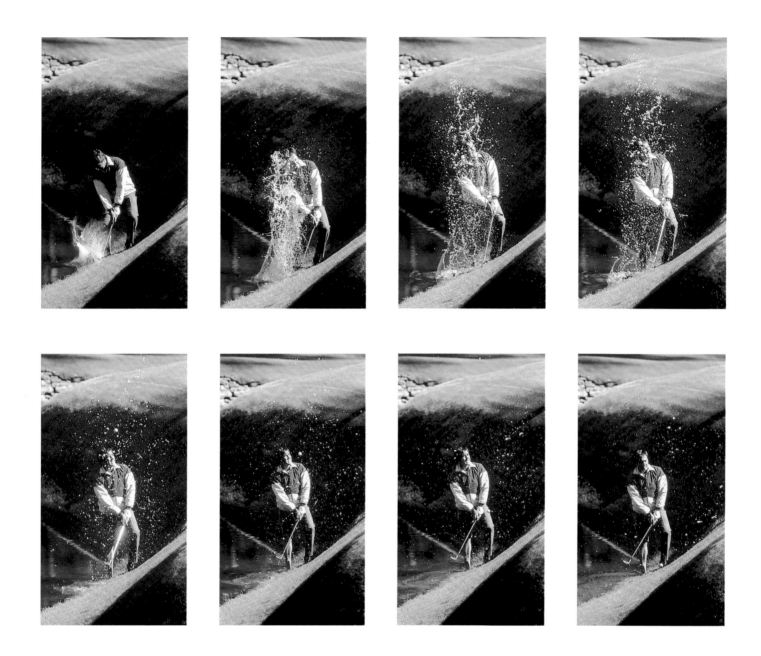

Not even Seve could wade into Rae's Creek and come out smelling of azaleas. David Cannon's picture sequence details one of the Spaniard's fabled watery duels at Augusta's notorious 13th hole.

Severiano Ballesteros visits Rae's Creek during the 1989 Masters

Photographs by David Cannon

Golf's Houdini caught in the act...

"*It was late afternoon on a typically hot Augusta day. I had been on the course with my 30 kilos of equipment since 7.15 am and I was shattered. From a distance I saw Seve playing his approach to the 13th and judging by the familiar body language I thought he might be in trouble. Was he in Rae's Creek? The only way to find out was to walk as fast as possible (no running here at Augusta) through the massed ranks of spectators (no photographers inside the ropes at Augusta) towards the green 400 yards away, I arrived to find Seve undoing his shoelaces; his ball was lying half in the water and he was going to try to play it. The light was glorious – sun and shadows – and all I had to decide was which camera and which lens to use. In 1989 I was still using the original Canon FD system and was carrying the unique Canon Highspeed camera which would give me 14 pictures per second. Used with the 300ml f2.8 lens, it produced the results shown on these pages. The only disappointment was that Seve couldn't pull off one of his famous Houdini-like escapes, but for me, the struggle to reach the green had been well worthwhile. Without the effort, and the knowledge of Seve's body language I would have missed this sequence. If only the golfers knew the way we rattle the bones to put their balls into places that will give us images such as these!*"

DAVID CANNON

"And the meek shall inherit the earth"

PETER ALLISS

*A*ugusta National, where dreams are made and hearts are broken.
   Larry Mize celebrates after his miraculous chip-in to defeat Greg Norman
   in the 1987 Masters play-off; utter despair for Tom Lehman as his eagle attempt
   at the 15th slips past the hole during the final round of the 1994 Masters.

Larry Mize wins the 1987 Masters (above)

Tom Lehman's agony at the 1994 Masters (right)

PHOTOGRAPHS BY DAVID CANNON

The photographer's
bag of tricks…

"*I use the Canon EOS
system as the basis of my
camera equipment, and
on the final day of a major
tournament I usually
carry three cameras – two
EOS 1s and an EOS 5.
The EOS 5 has a very
quiet shutter which is
ideal for golf where
camera noise is a very
sensitive area! I carry a
number of lenses including
the Canon EF 600ml f4
as my 'long lens', the
Canon EF 200ml f1.8
and various 'short lenses'
including the super-wide
14ml f2.8 for the scenic
and atmospheric shots.
The moral behind
carrying this amount
of equipment is that
'Murphy's law' is bound
to strike three miles from
the clubhouse and you
find you haven't brought
the one lens you need
for a specific shot.*"

DAVID CANNON

"*My victory in the 1992 US Open has to be the absolute highlight of my golfing career. This wonderful photograph recalls what was probably the worst shot of my final round – I was getting ready to hit a 'shank' right of the 9th green!*"

TOM KITE

*W*hy let the facts spoil a good picture? Tom Kite mastered gale force winds at Pebble Beach to win his first Major championship. Blurred vision for Dr Gil Morgan? He led by seven strokes half way through the third round before the proverbial wheels fell off.

Tom Kite at Pebble Beach (left)

Gil Morgan loses his way (above)

PHOTOGRAPHS BY DAVID CANNON

*"What does this picture mean to me?
The only word that comes into my head is 'Yessss!'"*

Payne Stewart

*P*ayne Stewart won the US Open at Hazeltine in 1991 after a tense play-off with Scott Simpson. Stewart appeared set to win a second championship two years later at Baltusrol, until Lee Janzen revived memories of Tom Watson at Pebble Beach in 1982 by chipping-in for a birdie two at the 70th hole.

Payne Stewart at the 1991 US Open (left)

Lee Janzen chips-in at Baltusrol in the 1993 US Open (right)

Photographs by David Cannon

The 1993 Open Championship at Royal St George's was a classic. When Nick Faldo birdied the 18th for a course record 63 in the second round, it looked as if he might successfully defend his Open crown. Faldo went out in the final pairing on Sunday and scored a 67 but Greg Norman produced the performance of a lifetime, shooting a brilliant 64 to eclipse his great rival.

Nick Faldo (left)

Greg Norman (above)

PHOTOGRAPHS BY DAVID CANNON

"One day you will be champion"

SEVERIANO BALLESTEROS AT THE CONCLUSION OF THE 1988 OPEN CHAMPIONSHIP

AT ROYAL LYTHAM AND ST ANNE'S

With a gutsy birdie at the 70th hole, an extra-ordinary eagle at the 71st and a safe par at the final hole, Nick Price realised Ballesteros' prophecy.
"I had my left hand on the trophy in 1982, my right hand on it in 1988 and now I have both hands on the trophy… and boy it feels great!"

Nick Price plays to the 72nd at Turnberry (opposite)
<small>Photograph by Stephen Munday</small>

Unusual viewing at the Open Championship (above left)
<small>Photograph by David Cannon</small>

The Open trophy (left)
<small>Photograph by Dan Smith</small>

*J*ohn Daly amazed himself and stunned the golfing
world by winning the 1991 USPGA Championship
at Crooked Stick. Greg Norman's putt to win the
1993 championship at Inverness appeared to hit
the centre of the hole but spun around the cup
and stayed above ground. He lost the resulting
play-off to Paul Azinger.

John Daly (above)
Photograph by Stephen Munday

Greg Norman (right)
Photograph by Gary Newkirk

"That has to be one of the nastiest lip-outs you will ever see"

<small>Paul Azinger, who profited from Greg Norman's near miss</small>

EUROPE

Agony for Bernhard Langer (and Europe) at Kiawah Island

Photograph by David Cannon

EUROPE

by Mitchell Platts

THE SCENARIO was laced with romance, loaded with reality. Bernhard Langer's ambivalent affair with the most important club in the bag – his putter – was legendary, and the golfing gods had decreed him to face the ultimate stroke. If he holed the six footer on the last green at Kiawah Island then Europe would retain the Ryder Cup. It was a twist of fate torn from the manuscript of a masochistic novelist.

We all craned our necks to watch that day and, yes, prayed. Bernard Gallacher, Europe's captain, bit his lip, and prayed. Seve Ballesteros squinted, and prayed. Nick and Sam, Ollie and Woosie clenched their fists, and prayed. Meanwhile if there was hope and faith in the hearts of every European then surely there was a grain of charity amongst the American opposition. For Bernhard Langer is a man of the game, respected by his peers and by all who love the ancient game, and recognised as one of the finest ambassadors for the PGA European Tour.

His story is an intoxicating mix of triumph and tragedy. He was nine years old when he started to caddie at the Augsberg Golf Club in the village of Burgwalden, a five mile walk from the family home in the village of Anheusen, and not much older when he revealed to his friends his ambition to be a professional golfer. "They all thought I was mad", he recalls.

Langer, however, learned quickly, progressing as an assistant professional in Munich, and then in 1976 he drove to the south of Spain to prepare for a first year on the PGA European Tour. His limited funds compelled him to stay in fleabag-accommodation, and he refused in one to turn on the light at night because the floor was filthy and the wallpaper hung loose. He missed the cut that week, and the next.

Yet Langer's resolve, soon to become legendary, kept him going. His piercing, iceberg blue eyes resembled those of Nicklaus. His inner strength stemmed from a determination to succeed not only for personal glory but also for nationalistic pride. The boy who grew up with the powdery smell of cement from the overalls of his father Erwin, who made his living building houses, wanted to lay the foundations of a new Germany at least as far as golf was concerned. What is more he possessed the power to propel the ball such prodigious distances that it seemed conceivable that this son of a bricklayer could become a sporting hero.

There was, however, a spiteful intruder. As a teenager, Langer was razor sharp on the greens. Seven foot putts were regarded as "gimmes". Then came the yips, that veritable demon which afflicts most in time but few at such a young age. Langer, however, had the

Severiano Ballesteros putts on the 17th green at Gleneagles, Scotland ("Europe", pages 54-55)

PHOTOGRAPH BY DAVID CANNON

strength of character to exorcise the demon. He won the Cacharel Under-25 Championship in Nimes in 1979 by 17 strokes – slotting home every putt imaginable. "I couldn't stop laughing ", he recalled. "Even when I hit a bad putt the ball bounced off a footprint or a spike mark and went in." From there he carried on winning. The 1980 Dunlop Masters, the 1981 German Open. The Casio World Open in Japan in 1983. His extraordinary capacity to handle adversity was becoming well known, as was his reputation for being a man of integrity and instinctive honesty. So it was that he passed what to most observers was the true examination specifically of his putting stroke, when on the contoured greens at Augusta National he won the 1985 Masters. He would continue to win, both in Europe and around the world, although the yips would reappear to further test his resolve. Langer, however, could cope with that and more.

But now, he stood over that famous six foot putt at Kiawah Island. Hale Irwin, his opponent in the singles, stood back. If Langer holed he would win, the match would be halved and as the holders Europe would retain Sam Ryder's elegant golden chalice. David Cannon was ready to capture the moment, one of cliched ecstasy or agony. The silence was eerie.

The putt of course, missed by the cruellest fraction in the history of the Ryder Cup. Langer, as Cannon's picture clearly shows, froze; his face contorted in anguish. Later, inevitably, there were tears. He cried, so did others. And with good reason. Gallacher said no one should be put under that pressure. Seve said that not a player in the world would have holed that putt that day.

What mattered most, of course, was what Langer, a tolerant Born Again Christian, thought. "I had such good feelings about that putt. I was calm. I'd played increasingly better as the round wore on. I felt encouraged inside myself. I knew the magnitude of it, but I was in control. Then the ball just slid past. In a way, maybe it was good that it was me in that position. It's not easy being a loser, but the faith I have helps me to put things like that in perspective. I actually got over it quickly."

So this mild-mannered, meticulous man, whose demeanour on-course can be thoroughly mesmerising, returned home where the very next week he won the German Masters. It was nothing less than anyone expected. As one of the most analytical of golfers in the history of the game, no player is better armed to put fate behind him and face the future with the overt awareness that the game offers no certainty that such moments can be consigned to the past. Rather they remain as a constant reminder that those twin imposters, triumph and tragedy, are always around the next dog-leg.

Bernhard Langer was most certainly aware of that once again at Augusta National in 1993. This time, however, there was good reason for him to celebrate as he walked the last few yards to the 18th green, lifted his left arm to the spectators and then prepared to putt. He held a five shot lead. His first putt rolled a few inches past the hole. Langer, with a twinkle in his eye, turned to the gallery. "Is that good?" Then he tapped the ball softly into the cup and prepared to put on the Green Jacket for the second time in his life.

Mitchell Platts is the Director of Communications, PGA European Tour

Re-dressing the balance. Just a little over 18 months after his experience at Kiawah Island, Bernhard Langer was donning his second Masters Green Jacket. Langer cruised to victory at Augusta, winning by four strokes from Chip Beck. It was the eighth time in fourteen years that a European player had won.

Bernhard Langer, 1993 Masters

PHOTOGRAPH BY STEPHEN MUNDAY

*A*fter a decade of promise, Swedish golfers are now making a major impact on European golf. Two of the country's best young players are Per-Ulrik Johansson and Joakim Haeggman. In 1993 Haeggman became the first Swede to play in the Ryder Cup.

Per-Ulrik Johansson (left)
PHOTOGRAPH BY DAVID CANNON

Joakim Haeggman (below)
PHOTOGRAPH BY HOWARD BOYLAN

Golf in Europe is played on a very cosmopolitan stage. In fact, it is not unusual for the leaderboard at a PGA European Tour event to comprise players from four or five continents and a dozen or more countries.

Eduardo Romero (main picture)
PHOTOGRAPH BY STEPHEN MUNDAY

Anders Forsbrand (top left)

PHOTOGRAPH BY DAVID CANNON

Tony Johnstone (below left)

PHOTOGRAPH BY DAVID CANNON

Frank Nobilo (top right)

PHOTOGRAPH BY DAVID CANNON

Christy O'Connor Jnr (below right)

PHOTOGRAPH BY STEPHEN MUNDAY

Latin temperament on show in Britain: Argentinian golfer Vicente Fernandez throws his putter in the air and leaps for joy after holing a huge winning putt in the 1992 English Open at The Belfry. Vicente, however, forgot one golden rule – what goes up must come down! Spain's José-Maria Olazabal shows his frustration as a putt shaves the hole (and finishes directly behind it) in the 1991 Scottish Open at Gleneagles.

Vicente Fernandez (left)
Photographs by Stephen Munday

José-Maria Olazabal (right)
Photograph by David Cannon

Silent and thoughtful. A ponderous Ian Woosnam tries to figure out his poor form during the 1991 Ryder Cup at Kiawah Island. Severiano Ballesteros in action at the Spanish Open. Silencio? Are they serious? You cannot silence a Ballesteros.

Ian Woosnam (left)

<small>Photograph by Simon Bruty</small>

Severiano Ballesteros (below)

<small>Photograph by Stephen Munday</small>

T wo of Europe's transatlantic stars: Sweden's Liselotte Neumann
and England's Trish Johnson are among a select group of players
who successfully divide their time between the burgeoning
WPG European Tour and the more established LPGA Tour.

Liselotte Neumann (above left)

Trish Johnson (above right)

PHOTOGRAPHS BY DAVID CANNON

*G*reat friends and great team mates: Alison Nicholas and Laura Davies, both former winners of the Weetabix Women's British Open
have formed a formidable partnership for Europe in the Solheim Cup. Davies, of course, has become something of a golfing phenomenon.
Long regarded as the mightiest hitter in women's golf, she has become a multiple winner in all corners of the globe, has two LPGA Major
titles to her name and in 1994 established a huge lead at the top of the Ping Leaderboard, the women's world rankings.

Alison Nicholas (above)
PHOTOGRAPH BY RICHARD SAKER

Laura Davies (above right)
PHOTOGRAPH BY DAVID CANNON

'*Monty*' *shadows his mentor. The extraordinary resolve that has guided Nick Faldo to the pinnacle of world golf is not only admired by Colin Montgomerie – it is being emulated.*

Nick Faldo (above)

PHOTOGRAPH BY DAVID CANNON

Colin Montgomerie (right)

PHOTOGRAPH BY STEPHEN MUNDAY

*R*ain rarely stops play in golf but often it can reflect a mood.
Sandy Lyle and Steven Richardson: both are big and strong,
both are extremely gifted, but neither could win his place
in Europe's last Ryder Cup team.

Sandy Lyle (above)

Steven Richardson (right)

Photographs by David Cannon

AMERICA

by Rick Reilly

The unthinkable thought. The undoable done. The unwritable written. The undreamed lived.

Sunday 4.13.86. The 50th Masters. Forty-six years. Five shots back. Ten to play.

No majors in six years. No wins in two. One-hundred-sixtieth on the money list. Behind Don Halldorson. Ceremonial Golfer. The living legend. Wave to the people. Catch a Friday night flight. The great man. Standing right over there. Remember?

But wait a minute. Hold on a second.

Three on 9. Birdie. Three on 10. Birdie. Three on 11. Birdie. Four on 12. Bogie. Four on 13. Birdie. Three back.

Men climbing trees. Vendors leaving posts. Women breaking heels. Tears clouding sight. Sons reading putts.

The 14th, parred. The 15th, eagled. Two back.

Those green pants. That yellow shirt. That fading eyesight. That Godzilla putter. The Japanese driver. Those ungodly irons.

A 5-iron at 16. A deal with the devil. A ball that nearly disappears. A kick-in birdie.

A script you couldn't sell. One back.

Seve goes splash. Watson waves goodbye. Langer trips up. Young men. Young greens. Young game. Is this happening? Even.

Right here. Right now. 17th hole. Fifteen feet. Mouths cotton-dry. Voices gravel-spent. Palms sweat-soaked. Chills joy-riding.

Let it roll. Wiggle left. Wiggle right. Chase it to the hole. Raise that putter. Miracles happen. One ahead.

One last par. One last thunderclap. One last hug. Two last chances.

Tom Kite and a hole that won't stay put. Greg Norman and a 4-iron that won't listen. Jack Nicklaus and a destiny that won't swerve.

Thirty shots. Nine holes. Sixty-five. Forty-two regular. Six jackets. 20 majors.

The truest putt. The finest moment. The clearest day. The greatest player.

Remember?

Rick Reilly is a Senior Writer
for Sports Illustrated, USA

Jack Nicklaus birdies the 71st hole at the 1986 Masters (left)
PHOTOGRAPHS BY DAVID CANNON

Payne Stewart hits into a February sun at Pebble Beach ("America", pages 74-75)
PHOTOGRAPH BY STEPHEN DUNN

*F*red Couples appears heaven
blessed. He is laid back
and handsome, hugely
popular and enormously
talented. And his golf ball
can defy the laws of
gravity. Couples has
enjoyed team success,
both in the Ryder Cup
and the World Cup and
achieved personal glory
at Augusta by winning
the 1992 Masters.

Fred Couples during
the 1991 Ryder Cup at
Kiawah Island (above)
PHOTOGRAPH BY SIMON BRUTY

Fred Couples during
the 1993 World Cup
at Lake Nona (below)
PHOTOGRAPH BY STEPHEN MUNDAY

Fred Couples at the
12th hole, Augusta in
the 1992 Masters (opposite)
PHOTOGRAPH BY DAVID CANNON

If occasionally he appears to have lost his way – both on and off the course – there is no bigger draw in world golf than John Daly. The crowds love his no-nonsense, 'grip it and rip it' approach and they whoop and holler every time he smashes a 300 yards-plus drive

**John Daly at
Pebble Beach** (left)
PHOTOGRAPH BY STEPHEN DUNN

John Daly at The Masters
(above right)
PHOTOGRAPH BY DAVID CANNON

**John Daly at Noordwijkse
in the Heineken Dutch
Open** (right)
PHOTOGRAPH BY DAVID CANNON

*W*hen they played Walker Cup golf together their ambitions were very diverse: left-hander Phil Mickelson was the outstanding prodigy, merely biding his time before he amassed Major championships in Nicklaus-like fashion, and Jay Sigel the hugely experienced campaigner, the veteran of numerous Walker Cups and a double US Amateur champion. Now they are both rising stars – Mickelson on the PGA Tour and Sigel (so much for the career amateur!) on the PGA Senior Tour.

Phil Mickelson (left)

Jay Sigel (right)

PHOTOGRAPHS BY DAVID CANNON

Riding the gravy train: 'Super Mex' and the super seniors. Lee Trevino, Ray Floyd and (hiding behind his towel) Japan's Isao Aoki are three former champions now enjoying life on the PGA Senior Tour. When Trevino approached 50 he joked that he was going to acquire a giant-sized wheelbarrow, one sufficiently large to transport to the bank all the hundreds of thousands of dollars that he would win on the over-50s circuit. The same wheelbarrow must now be buckling under the weight.

Isao Aoki (above left)
PHOTOGRAPH BY DAVID CANNON

Lee Trevino (below left)
PHOTOGRAPH BY STEPHEN MUNDAY

Ray Floyd (opposite)
PHOTOGRAPH BY DAVID CANNON

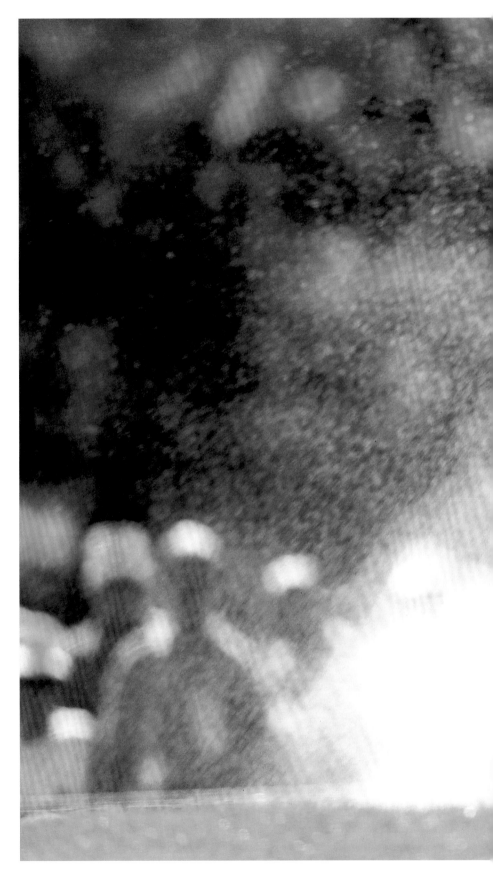

Striking images and contrasting personalities from the LPGA Tour. All three players have won Major titles: fiery Dottie Mochrie (whose maiden name somewhat appropriately was Pepper) finally realised her potential when she captured the Dinah Shore tournament in 1992; Lauri Merten was a surprise, though hugely popular winner of the 1993 US Women's Open (her first victory in nine years) while Patty Sheehan has become one of the legends of the women's game, winning five Majors and a place in the LPGA Hall of Fame.

Dottie Mochrie
(far left, top)

Patty Sheehan
(far left, below)

Lauri Merten (left)

PHOTOGRAPHS BY DAVID CANNON

*T*he A-Z of American golf: Paul Azinger looks relaxed
as he poses for the camera, but he normally plays
with great intensity. Fuzzy Zoeller, on the other
hand, rarely appears to be anything but relaxed!
As for the next US Ryder Cup captain,
Lanny Wadkins, he always wears his
heart on his sleeve

Lanny Wadkins (left)

Paul Azinger (above top)

Fuzzy Zoeller (above lower)

PHOTOGRAPHS BY DAVID CANNON

REST OF THE WORLD

Thaworn Wiratchant

PHOTOGRAPH BY DAVID CANNON

REST OF THE WORLD

by Spencer Robinson

IN HIS NATIVE Thailand, Thaworn Wiratchant is known, simply, as 'Strong Wind, No Play'. Lean as a beanpole, it is easy to understand why. Legend has it that the nickname was coined more than a decade ago while Thaworn, then in his mid-teens, was competing in a junior tournament in unusually unpleasant conditions.

Each time Thaworn addressed the ball, his slight frame fought valiantly to withstand the battering from fierce winds. Weighing barely 120 pounds, it was one battle he could not win. Like a flagstick swaying wildly on a blustery day on a Scottish links, Thaworn wilted from the midriff. He does not remember his score that day; only that he could not wait to finish the round.

Like most Asian golfers, Thaworn is more comfortable in scorching heat and blistering humidity. Wind, rain and freezing temperatures are no friend to Asian players. Fortunately for Thaworn and his compatriots it is rare to experience such alien weather conditions in Thailand.

On the sun-baked fairways of Southeast Asia, Thaworn, now aged 27, is a formidable golfer, and make no mistake. He began winning tournaments when he was in his early teens, earning a reputation as a prodigious talent. In 1985, he won the Hong Kong Open Amateur Championship over the Eden Course at Fanling. It was his first success outside Thailand. Twelve months later he returned to the Royal Hong Kong Golf Club's Garden of Eden and helped his country to an historic victory in the Putra Cup, the Southeast Asian team championship.

There is little in either his physical appearance or demeanour to suggest that Thaworn is a golfing hero to tens of thousands of people. But in Bangkok, Chiang Mai, Phuket and Pattaya, and all points north, south, west and east in the Land of Smiles, he is just that.

Thaworn is blessed with the engaging friendly facial features that are so typical of the Thais. His golf swing, however, could not be described as a thing of beauty. On the contrary. Western golfing gurus would cringe at his inimitable self-taught 'style', the like of which you won't find in any golf manual in any corner of the globe.

Pretty on the eye it is not. His slender arms flail in a windmill-like manner that makes purists wince. Blink and you may miss it! Yet despite an idiosyncratic movement of the right arm and a flourishing, exaggerated follow-through, at the moment of impact Thaworn succeeds in getting the club face square to the ball. Coupled with exceptional club-head speed, he is able to propel the ball respectable distances. John Daly he most definitely is not,

Greg Norman in Japan
("Rest of the World" pages 90-91)

PHOTOGRAPH BY ANTON WANT

but wielding his carbon-shafted driver to good effect it's not often that Thaworn strays too far from the short grass. And therein lies one of the secrets of his success.

As a professional golfer, Thaworn has represented his country in Johnnie Walker Classics, World Cups and, most notably, the Alfred Dunhill Cup when in 1991 he was a member of the Thai team that won through to the finals at the Home of Golf.

For the second year in succession, Thailand were afforded the dubious privilege of being drawn against England in the first round. While Sukree Oncham faced Paul Broadhurst and Boonchu Ruangkit squared off with Steven Richardson, Thaworn drew the short straw. He had to take on Nick Faldo.

There was to be no fairytale story. Thailand were whitewashed. Sukree and Boonchu shot 77s and were soundly beaten by their opponents in the medal-matchplay format. Thaworn, against all odds, had briefly threatened to pull off one of the tournament's biggest upsets. Out in 37 he trailed the Englishman by just one. Eventually, though, he finished with a 75 and lost by six.

Throughout that contest, biting winds swirled in mischievously from the North Sea, while a menacing blanket of fog wrapped itself around the famed St Andrews links. Thaworn neither felt at home, nor looked it. Emerging from the gloom on to the first tee, Thaworn was clad in a strikingly unfamiliar white waterproof suit. For the entire round a bobble hat was pulled way down over his ears, concealing the top of his head. Had it not been for that distinctive swing even his countrymen would not have recognised him.

Three years on and the memories of that Scottish adventure still linger. "It was not pleasant," said Thaworn, shivering at the bitter recollection as he paused between hitting balls on the driving range of the Royal Thai Army Golf Course on the outskirts of bustling Bangkok. Glancing upwards to the golden sun beating down from clear blue skies, he added: "But it was an experience I will never forget."

Spencer Robinson is the Managing Editor of The Asian Golfer

*H*ave clubs will travel. There is no greater exponent of golfing wanderlust
than talented Fijian player Vijay Singh. A winner in Europe and America,
not to mention 'the rest of the world', it is often claimed that no professional
practises harder… the Gary Player of his generation?

Vijay Singh

Photograph by David Cannon

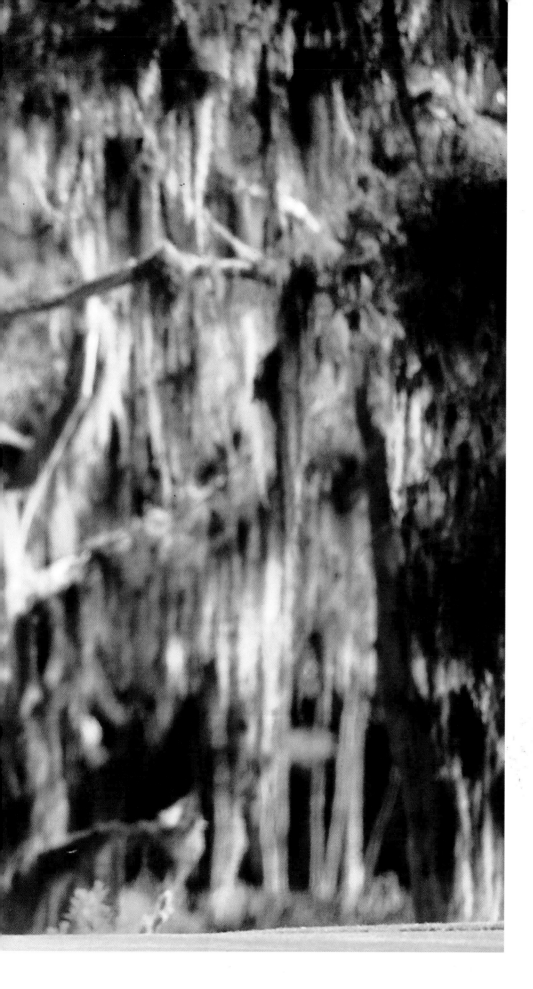

*A World Cup in Lake Nona,
Florida and a World
Championship in Tryall,
Jamaica – no wonder Henry
Longhurst used to say, 'Golf takes
us to such beautiful places'.
Mark McNulty plays from the
18th fairway at Lake Nona
and Nick Faldo finds
an appealing 19th hole to
celebrate his victory at Tryall.*

**Nick Faldo, winner of
the 1992 Johnnie Walker
World Championship** (above)

**Mark McNulty at Lake Nona in the
1993 Heineken World Cup** (left)

PHOTOGRAPHS BY DAVID CANNON

*W*hen the 1992 Australian Open was held at
The Lakes in Sydney hazards appeared in all shapes
and sizes. Eventual winner, Steve Elkington is
pictured playing from a beautifully manicured
fairway bunker while fellow Australian
Peter Senior seems totally oblivious to
the aeroplane passing overhead.

Steve Elkington (left)
PHOTOGRAPH BY STEPHEN MUNDAY

Peter Senior (above)
PHOTOGRAPH BY JOE MANN

To whom it may N... [illegible handwritten inscription]
Best Wishes Good Golfing
in 1995.
[signature]

*Visions in green and gold. Australians
Mike Harwood (the one sporting the patriotic
Ken Done tee shirt) and Robert Allenby
(widely regarded as the most promising
Antipodean golfer since Greg Norman).*

Mike Harwood (left) AKA Graham Watson

Robert Allenby (above)

PHOTOGRAPHS BY DAVID CANNON

When he's not winning Major championships, heading US PGA Tour Money Lists or strolling to victory in Million Dollar Challenges, Nick Price likes to fish near his home in Orlando, Florida. Of course, it is most convenient that some of the best local fishing is to be found nearby at Lake Nona and that this just happens to be where friend and guru David Leadbetter resides.

Nick Price

Photographs by David Cannon

*M*eet the new 'star of Africa'. Ernie Els has the golfing
world at his feet. Here he is pictured at home and at
the 'office'. The home is in Germiston, Johannesburg
and the golf course is Baltusrol, New Jersey
where the young South African gained a top ten
finish on his US Open debut. Twelve months later
he was the US Open champion.

Ernie Els in the 1993 US Open at Baltusrol (left)
PHOTOGRAPH BY GARY NEWKIRK

Ernie Els relaxes at home in South Africa (above)
PHOTOGRAPH BY DAVID CANNON

There are times when golf in Japan can seem a very close-knit family affair. All three Ozaki brothers, 'Joe', 'Jet' and the mighty 'Jumbo' win regularly on the Japanese Tour. 'Jumbo', more properly Masashi is the superstar – a legend indeed. He has won more tournaments in Japan than Jack Nicklaus has won in America and the Japanese golfing public idolises him in much the way that Americans worship Arnold Palmer. For the past two decades 'Jumbo' has been the country's greatest player although both Tsuneyuki 'Tommy' Nakajima and Isao Aoki have occasionally threatened his hegemony. Together, they certainly represent 'The Big Three' of Japanese golf.

Naomichi 'Joe' Ozaki (above left)
PHOTOGRAPH BY DAVID CANNON

Tateo 'Jet' Ozaki (above centre)
PHOTOGRAPH BY SIMON BRUTY

Masashi 'Jumbo' Ozaki (above right)
PHOTOGRAPH BY DAVID CANNON

Tsuneyuki 'Tommy' Nakajima (left)
PHOTOGRAPH BY DAVID CANNON

'Joe' Ozaki
at Augusta (above)

Isao Aoki (left)

Photographs by
Stephen Munday

*W*ell, what would you do if it cost £100,000 or more just to join a golf club?

'Driving range golf' is the only form of golf for millions of Japanese.

The three tiered Shiba range in Tokyo is the largest in the world.

The Shiba Golf Range, Tokyo (left)

The drive-in drive-over experience at the Shinjuku Range (above)

<small>PHOTOGRAPHS BY PASCAL RONDEAU</small>

*A*ll *the caddy can do is
stand and watch.
The Johnnie Walker
Classic has become the
biggest golf event in
Southeast Asia, attracting
truly international fields
and visiting such countries
as Thailand, Singapore,
Hong Kong and
(in 1995) the Philippines.
Bernhard Langer
experiences Kiawah
Island-type agony as his
chip narrowly misses
during the 1994 event
at the Blue Canyon
Country Club in Phuket,
Thailand.*

**Caddy at the 1994 Johnnie
Walker Classic** (left)

Bernhard Langer (right)

PHOTOGRAPHS BY DAVID CANNON

MATCHPLAY GOLF

Jim Milligan chips-in at the 17th to set up his famous victory
over Jay Sigel in the 1989 Walker Cup

PHOTOGRAPH BY DAVID CANNON

MATCHPLAY GOLF

by John Hopkins

MY HEART is hopelessly lost, not just to someone I won't stop to tell you about now, if you don't mind, but to matchplay golf. To my mind matchplay golf and international team events, men or women, amateur or professional, require everything that is good about sport. Head to head competition in a team event calls for courage, strategy, nerve and skill.

Let me call my witnesses. We are at Peachtree Golf Club in Atlanta on a sultry summer afternoon in 1989, the second day of the Walker Cup. The 1980s have been a rich time for supporters of European golf. Victory in a Ryder Cup at home in 1985 and then victory in a Ryder Cup in the US in 1987. And in between these historic events, a first, unexpected success in the Curtis Cup in America.

We are on the 15th green during the afternoon singles, and the match is absolutely poised. GB & I had led 11-5 at lunchtime but now there is barely the width of a cigarette paper between the two teams.

It's all down to Jim Milligan in his match against Jay Sigel, the last on the course, the destiny of the Walker Cup depending on the result. My first sight of the Scot came as he holed from eight feet to win the 15th and what I saw was this: a tall, broad-shouldered man with curly hair. He had a full swing that looked

firm under pressure and a wide putting stance. His face, even in the heat of a Southern summer, was pale with tension.

Milligan won the 16th to be only one down. He might have felt the pressure before but it was as nothing to what he felt now. Matchplay in a team competition is the ultimate test. Team mates depend on you. They can see your courage or lack of it. There are no hiding places. Make a mistake in strokeplay and you let yourself down, lose a few thousand pounds. Make a mistake in a team event and your error is compounded by the feelings of your disappointed affected colleagues. You have let them down, too.

On the 17th Milligan fluffed a chip from the back of the green, attempting to finesse a shot out of the clinging grass. Then Sigel made a hash of his. Then Milligan chipped in. Almost all his colleagues had gathered around the green and as he raised his clenched fist to acknowledge his dexterity, they, too, rose to acknowledge him.

All square with one to play and the Walker Cup depending on it. So far we had seen some courageous golf by Milligan. Now came some inspired captaincy by Geoff Marks. He took Milligan away from the 18th tee and talked to him intently. "Make him wait" Marks urged. "It's your honour. You take your time." He paused and looked straight into Milligan's

Ryder Cup scoreboard at The Belfry, 1993
("Matchplay Golf" pages 112-113)

PHOTOGRAPH BY DAVID CANNON

eyes. "Just get it on the fairway", he said. "Sigel's as nervous as a kitten and he'll crack."

A resolute drive by Milligan found the fairway, his second the side of the green. Sigel, as nervous as Marks had said, was on the edge of the green in two. Sensible matchplay demands you react to your animate opponent, not as in strokeplay, to a figure printed in black on a white card. Milligan watched as Sigel jerked at another chip, like a man holding an electric cattle prod. The ball hardly moved. Then he hit it to 25 feet.

Now the score was irrelevant. Milligan just had to take one fewer stroke and GB & I

would win the Walker Cup by one point. He did just that, taking heed of the maxim that if you have two for it you take them.

It was the most courageous 45 minutes of golf I have ever seen, just about the most exciting as well. I did not speak to Milligan after this remarkable performance and I have not spoken to him since. But I take my hat off to him. To my way of thinking he provided me with *the* moment in golf in a decade that was full of them.

Thanks Jim.

John Hopkins is golf correspondent of The Times

Milligan is engulfed by his jubilant team mates.

PHOTOGRAPH BY DAVID CANNON

*Y*ou can almost smell the salty air. The classic links at Rye is the
venue for one of the more eccentric annual matchplay golf events,
the President's Putter. Perhaps 'eccentric' is unfair for with a
field comprised of Oxford and Cambridge Blues it is always very
keenly contested – but to stage a major amateur tournament
on the English coast in January?

Winter golf at Rye
Photograph by Howard Boylan

*T*he 18th green at The Belfry is where Ryder Cups
have been won, lost and retained. Sam Torrance
(who holed the winning putt) in 1985 and
Christy O'Connor Jnr (who struck a famous 2-iron)
in 1989 savour their moments of glory.

**Christy O'Connor, 1989 Ryder Cup
by Johnnie Walker** (left)
PHOTOGRAPH BY BOB MARTIN

**Sam Torrance, 1985 Ryder Cup
by Johnnie Walker** (above)
PHOTOGRAPH BY DAVID CANNON

It has been described as the greatest partnership in the history of the Ryder Cup. Severiano Ballesteros and José-Maria Olazabal (alias 'Seve and Ollie') were first paired together at Muirfield Village in 1987. Matchplay golf, especially when the opposition is American, seems to bring the best out of both of them and when they are inspired they are almost invincible.

Ballesteros and Olazabal at Muirfield Village, 1987 Ryder Cup (above left)

PHOTOGRAPH BY SIMON BRUTY

Ballesteros and Olazabal at The Belfry, 1989 Ryder Cup by Johnnie Walker (below left)

PHOTOGRAPH BY SIMON BRUTY

Ballesteros and Olazabal at Kiawah Island, 1991 Ryder Cup (above right)

PHOTOGRAPH BY DAVID CANNON

Ballesteros and Olazabal at The Belfry, 1993 Ryder Cup by Johnnie Walker (below right)

PHOTOGRAPH BY SIMON BRUTY

*S*panish pride and Spanish passion: Ballesteros and Olazabal.

May their sun never set.

Played 15: Won 11, Halved 2, Lost 2

PHOTOGRAPH BY CHRIS COLE

*E*urope's finest hour? On a course designed by Jack Nicklaus and against a side led by Jack Nicklaus the team from the 'Old World' gained its first ever Ryder Cup triumph on American soil. Brilliantly captained by Tony Jacklin, with Seve Ballesteros as an inspirational lieutenant Europe produced a stunning performance to win at Muirfield Village, Ohio in 1987.

Severiano Ballesteros and Tony Jacklin embrace at Muirfield Village, 1987 Ryder Cup (above left)
PHOTOGRAPH BY SIMON BRUTY

The party they couldn't stop: Europeans celebrate an historic victory in the 1987 Ryder Cup (left)
PHOTOGRAPH BY DAVID CANNON

*T*he tide finally turns. It was ten years since the US last won the Ryder Cup and as Bernhard Langer stood over a six foot putt on the 18th green of the final singles at Kiawah Island it looked as if 'Uncle Sam' might be foiled once again. But Langer missed his putt and pandemonium broke out. Hale Irwin, Langer's opponent was drenched in champagne and later his captain, Dave Stockton was dunked in the Atlantic.

US celebrations beside the 18th green at Kiawah Island, 1991 Ryder Cup (above right)

Dave Stockton is ceremonially dunked (right)

PHOTOGRAPHS BY SIMON BRUTY

One giant leap for the WPG European Tour. Comprehensively beaten in the inaugural Solheim Cup encounter at Lake Nona in 1990, Europe achieved a remarkable victory when Mickey Walker's team overcame their American opponents at Dalmahoy in October 1992. Earlier the same year, Great Britain and Ireland's amateurs defeated the United States in the Curtis Cup at Royal Liverpool, winning a thrilling contest on the final green of the final match.

European ecstasy at Dalmahoy (right)

Europe's victorious 1992 Solheim Cup team
(far right, above)
PHOTOGRAPHS BY DAVID CANNON

The Curtis Cup charge
(far right, below)
PHOTOGRAPH BY CARL CAROLAN

America's 'King of Matchplay'. To his friends he is Corey Pavin; to his matchplay opponents he is known as 'Crazy' Pavin. Pavin's reputation as a fearless (and fearsome) competitor was established in the 1991 Ryder Cup at Kiawah Island, and cemented two year's later when he played a key role in America's victory at The Belfry. Just a few weeks after that team success Pavin won the World Matchplay title at Wentworth, defeating home favourite Nick Faldo in the 36 hole final.

Corey Pavin at Kiawah Island, 1991 Ryder Cup (left)
<small>PHOTOGRAPH BY SIMON BRUTY</small>

Corey Pavin at the 1993 Toyota World Matchplay Championship, October 1993 (right)
<small>PHOTOGRAPHS BY DAVID CANNON</small>

An elated Zimbabwean and a triumphant team of Americans; a frozen Australian and a mist-enveloped Spaniard. Extraordinary light and weather at the Alfred Dunhill Cup on the Old Course at St Andrews.

USA, winners of the 1993 Alfred Dunhill Cup (top)
PHOTOGRAPH BY STEPHEN MUNDAY

Tony Johnstone, 1993 (left)

Greg Norman, 1992 (above left)
PHOTOGRAPHS BY DAVID CANNON

Severiano Ballesteros, 1988 (above right)
PHOTOGRAPH BY SIMON BRUTY

COURSES

4th hole, Royal County Down (top)

17th hole, Ballybunion (Old Course) (below)

COURSES

by Nick Edmund

YOU ARE A TIRED but very contented soul. For two weeks you have been golfing your way around the Emerald Isle and now you have reached the final hole of your final destination. You are on the 18th green of the Mahony's Point Course at Killarney in the south west of Ireland. You contemplate the splendour of the surroundings: the encircling mountains and hills; the lake, shimmering in the early evening sunlight, and the tall pines and rhododendrons that so gloriously frame the green. The only sound is the gentle lapping of Lough Leane. You are trying to line-up a 20 footer for a two – a wonderful way to finish your trip – but how can you concentrate in such a setting? You recall the words of Henry Longhurst, who on reaching this very green declared, 'What a wonderful place to die!' You start to wonder. And then your mind begins to wander…

You are in a clubhouse you do not recognise and a strange and slightly heated conversation is taking place between an Englishman, a Scotsman and an American. It seems that they have taken Longhurst's observation a step further and are actually discussing the likely character of the Heavenly Links. The Scotsman is insisting that it must be an exact replica of the Old Course at St Andrews – Valley of Sin included. The American is equally adamant that much of the course will resemble Augusta – Amen Corner

especially. As for the rather cantankerous Englishman, he is asserting that it must be a perfect copy of Royal St George's.

Then they notice you. You are summoned over and requested to adjudicate. Now, remember, for 14 days you have had Ireland on your mind and you are not overly impressed with the manner of these people, so you tell them straight. You advise them that when the time comes, they should put on their eternal plus fours and prepare themselves for nine holes at Royal County Down in Newcastle, followed by a back nine over the Old Course at Ballybunion.

Why the front nine at Newcastle? Well, for one thing, you fell in love with the place. This is where the purple and blue Mountains of Mourne sweep down to the sea. The golf links – and what a spectacular and rugged links you found – follows the curve of Dundrum Bay. Just as the rhododendrons were out at Killarney, so the gorse was in full bloom at Newcastle. The only parts of the course that didn't appear wrapped in gold were the emerald fairways and greens, the heather-clad dunes and the myriad bunkers with their wild, tussocky banks. You explain to the trio that they are likely to walk the first three holes backwards, so enchanted will they be with the view over their shoulder. But they will turn around properly at the short 4th and face the

Turnberry, 9th tee with Ailsa Craig
("Courses", pages 130-131)
PHOTOGRAPH BY DAVID ROGERS

mountains for the first time. They will see the massive peak of Slieve Donard dwarfing the town below, and they will need no more convincing as to the wisdom of your choice.

They will play some classic links holes after the 4th, and some very demanding ones. Not only has Royal County Down been described as the most beautiful golf course in the world but American Herbert Warren Wind once suggested it was the sternest examination in golf he had ever taken.

Concerned that the intrepid threesome might be more than a little spellbound by the time they leave the green at the magical 9th, you warn them they had better pull themselves together before tackling their back nine.

You recall thinking Ballybunion the most dramatic and thrilling golf course you had ever played. The front nine contained several good holes (a couple of modest ones too) but it was the back nine that really bowled you over. You couldn't believe how vast the sandhills were at Ballybunion, nor how extensive. This was truly life in the fast lane.

A pitch over a grassy valley to a plateau green at the 10th and you were right beside the Atlantic Ocean. From there on you rarely left the cliff edges, as exhilarating holes followed one after another. The 11th was an astonishing hole – huge dunes off to the left, the Atlantic to the right and a fairway that cascaded in natural terraces towards a distant windswept green perched beside the ocean; also the par three 15th, all 200 yards of it, down to a two tiered amphitheatre green. And as for the view from the elevated tee at the 17th – that was a sight you will never forget. You had never seen such a rollercoaster of a hole.

But as you prepare to head off down the hill at the 17th the images start to blur. Is it an excess of adrenaline? Or maybe you are beginning to worry how you might justify a blind finishing hole. Now you start to see some amazing visions... visions of golfers! Isn't that Jack Nicklaus in yellow on the 17th green, waving his putter in salute? And surely that's Jim Milligan chipping towards the flag? More familiar visions are standing beside the 18th tee, beckoning you to join them. Arnold Palmer tells you he is considering playing one more US Open; Thaworn Wiratchant, bless his cotton socks, is wearing a bobble hat; Seve promises he will birdie the final hole and Bernhard Langer assures you that this time he will make that putt…

That putt! Suddenly you come round. You are back on the 18th green at Killarney. The shadows have lengthened slightly but your 20 footer is still no nearer the hole. But you are now confident of the line and moments later it has disappeared – you made your two! With a spring in your step you are off to celebrate at the 19th hole. You now appreciate some of what Henry meant, and you know precisely why the locals call Killarney, 'Heaven's Reflex'.

Nick Edmund is the Editor of
Following the Fairways

*Several cities could claim to have more golf courses than Melbourne,
but surely none has as many great courses. The source of Melbourne's wealth
is the celebrated sand-belt and included amongst the riches are the 36 holes
(East and West Courses) at Royal Melbourne which, when combined
for championship purposes to produce the Composite Course,
creates one of the best 18 hole layouts in the world.*

5th hole, (Composite) Royal Melbourne Golf Club, Australia (above right)

16th hole, Victoria Golf Club, Melbourne, Australia (left)

10th hole, Kingston Heath Golf Club, Melbourne, Australia (below right)

<small>PHOTOGRAPHS BY DAVID CANNON</small>

If the State of Victoria can boast a near monopoly of Australia's finest 'traditional' courses then, equally, most of the country's best 'modern' designs are to be found on or near the Queensland coast. Fuelled by Japanese investment, the Gold Coast has witnessed the greatest amount of course building activity, however, a number of outstanding challenges have mushroomed in some extremely appealing locations right along the coast, as far north as Port Douglas.

Royal Pines, Gold Coast, Queensland (left)

Paradise Palms, Nr Cairns, Queensland (right)

Laguna Keys, Turtle Point, Queensland (above right)

PHOTOGRAPHS BY
STEPHEN MUNDAY

The finest golf links in England and the leading golf course in Spain. Royal Birkdale has staged the Ryder Cup twice, in 1965 and 1969, and Valderrama is due to stage the Ryder Cup in 1997.

3rd hole, Royal Birkdale GC
(left above)
PHOTOGRAPH BY STEPHEN MUNDAY

17th hole, Valderrama
(left below)
PHOTOGRAPH BY DAVID CANNON

Reds and yellows and pinks and greens, oranges and purples and blues.
Augusta is every golfer's rainbow; to win The Masters is to find
the pot of gold at the end of the rainbow.

9th hole, Augusta Par Three Course

PHOTOGRAPH BY DAVID CANNON

Muirfield Village has been described as Jack Nicklaus' baby: "the first course I built on my own", and he named it after the links where he won his first Open Championship. Each year the Memorial Tournament is played here and in 1987 Muirfield Village hosted the Ryder Cup. If there is a better conditioned and more manicured course in the world than Augusta, this is it.

5th hole, Muirfield Village, Columbus, Ohio
PHOTOGRAPH BY DAVID CANNON

*W*hat golf architects are
able to create nowadays
beggars belief. They can
carve and sculpt holes
in the Californian desert
and build beautiful
designs over reclaimed
swamps in Florida;
but can even their finest
efforts truly compare
with the handiwork of
Mother Nature?

17th hole, PGA West,
La Quinta, California
(left above)

3rd hole, Spyglass Hill,
Monterey, California
(left below)

9th hole, Pebble Beach,
Monterey, California
(right above)

5th hole, (East) Grand
Cypress Resort, Orlando,
Florida (right below)

PHOTOGRAPHS BY DAVID CANNON

*It is the 'Home of Golf': from the Swilcan Burn to the
Principal's Nose and from the Road Hole to the Valley of Sin,
history is everywhere at St Andrews. Bobby Jones once said,
"The more I studied the Old Course the more I loved it,
and the more I loved it the more I studied it."*

St Andrews (Old Course) (right)

The R & A Clubhouse, St Andrews (above)

PHOTOGRAPHS BY DAVID CANNON

*E*ast Sussex National and Mount Juliet are rivals for the unofficial
title of 'Best New Course in Great Britain and Ireland'.
Both are less than five years old, yet both already host
important PGA European Tour events – East Sussex
(where there are 36 holes) the European Open
and Mount Juliet, the Murphy's Irish Open.

18th hole, East Sussex National (East Course), England (left)

11th hole, Mount Juliet, Co Kilkenny, Ireland (above)

PHOTOGRAPHS BY DAVID CANNON

There is a timeless beauty about links golf. A quick glance at the two courses to the left and it is not instantly apparent which is the older. The reality is that one opened in 1993 (Pat Ruddy's spectacular design at Brittas Bay in Ireland) and the other staged the first Open Championship in 1860! Next to links golf, the British Isles is most renowned for its heathland layouts, especially the great cluster of courses situated south and west of London, where the likes of Sunningdale and Wentworth are found.

8th hole, The European Club, Brittas Bay, County Wicklow, Ireland (left above)

17th hole, Prestwick, Ayrshire, Scotland
(left below)

8th hole, Wentworth (West Course) Surrey, England
(right above)

5th and 6th holes, Sunningdale (Old Course) Surrey, England
(right below)

PHOTOGRAPHS BY DAVID CANNON

From browns to greens, then all sorts of colours. When it comes to discussing great golfing oases Dubai must have the last word. Not long ago there was only an 'ex-pats' club, where the greens were 'browns'; then came golf's extraordinary square kilometre, the Emirates Cub, and now two more courses have opened in Dubai – one of which specialises in floodlit golf!

The Opening Ceremony, Dubai Creek Golf and Yacht Club (left)

The 'original' Dubai Country Club (right above)

Aerial view of the Emirates Golf Club (right below)

Floodlit golf at Nad-al-Shiba Golf Club, Dubai (far right)

Photographs by David Cannon

*I*t has been described as South Africa's latest diamond.
The Lost City Golf Club at Sun City: a jewel of a golf course
carved out of a wild landscape by Gary Player.

Lost City Golf Club at Sun City, South Africa

PHOTOGRAPHS BY DAVID CANNON

*"Go placidly amid
the heather and gorse
and remember what
peace there may be
on the fairway"*

Alone on the Links

PHOTOGRAPH BY CHRIS COLE

Visions of Golf

The photographs in this book have been selected from the
extensive golf library of Allsport, the world's leading sports picture agency.
The photographs and their availability in all corners of the world
would not have been possible without the help of the following:
The Photographers, Picture Researchers, Darkroom Staff,
Picture Desk Operators, Accounts Staff, Clerical Staff
and everyone else in the Allsport offices at

ALLSPORT UK
3 Greenlea Park
Prince George's Road
London SW19 2JD

Tel: (081) 685 1010 • Fax: (081) 648 5240

ALLSPORT USA
Suite 300
320 Wilshire Boulevard
Santa Monica
CA 90401

Tel: (310) 395 2955 • Fax: (310) 394 6099

ALLSPORT NEW YORK
13B Gramercy Place
280 Park Avenue South
New York 10010

Tel: (212) 979 0903 • Fax: (212) 979 0460

and the international network of agencies
on all five continents.

Kensington West Productions Ltd
5 Cattle Market, Hexham
Northumberland NE46 1NJ

Tel: (0434) 609933 • Fax: (0434) 600066